MW00989665

*U*nderstanding
The One You Love

STEVE STEPHENS

HARVEST HOUSE PUBLISHERS
Eugene, Oregon 97402

Cover by Terry Dugan Design, Minneapolis, Minnesota
Author photo by Yuen Lui Studio, Clackamas, Oregon

Understanding the One You Love

Copyright © 1998 by Erroll E. Stephens, Jr.
Published by Harvest House Publishers
Eugene, Oregon 97402

Library of Congress Cataloging-in-Publication Data

Stephens, Steve.
    Understanding the one you love / Steve Stephens.
        p.   cm.
    ISBN 1-56507-815-2
    1. Marriage—Miscellanea. 2. Man-woman relationships—Miscellanea.
    3. Love—Miscellanea. 4. Communication in marriage—Miscellanea.
I. Title.
HQ734.S856   1998
306.7—dc21   97-41492
                                                        CIP

Printed in the United States of America.

98 99 00 01 02 / BP / 10 9 8 7 6 5 4 3 2 1

To
Mom and Dad
for always being there

Acknowledgments

Tami for working through these questions with me, again and again.

Sue, my mother-in-law, for her endless encouragement and for patiently typing this manuscript.

Chip MacGregor for his enthusiastic support, positive direction, and expert editing.

Carolyn McCready and all the professional, friendly, and godly people I've met at Harvest House—for seeing the possibilities of this work and for making it happen.

All the great couples who inspired these questions—Roy and Joyce, Gary and Debra, Greg and Karen, Dan and Sue, Jim and Allison, Dan and Shanni, Todd and Monica, Brian and Mary, Mike and Mary Alice, Rob and Vicki, Jim and Colleen, Nathan and Terri, Bob and Carolyn, Wes and Debbie, Ross and Connie, Scott and Debbie, Charlie and Becky, Rick and Debbie, Dale and Beth, James and Cynde, Jon and Jennifer . . . just to name a few.

Taking Care

It's very simple—
if you don't take care of it,
it won't last.

Think about
    your car
    your house
    your health
    your business
    your pet
If you don't do certain things,
    it breaks down
    or falls apart
    or dies.
When something is important to us
we treat it with respect
and do what needs
to be done
to maintain it.

At most weddings,
amidst the music and flowers,
a man and a woman
make enormous promises to
    love,
    honor, and
    cherish
each other until death divides them.

A year or two later,
amidst the pressures and demands of life,
the man and the woman
> hurt,
> frustrate, and
> neglect

each other in ways they swore
would never happen to them.

Marriage is a fragile treasure.
It needs our devoted attention
to nurture it
and protect it
and strengthen it
every single day.
This sacred relationship
does not grow without
difficult labor and selfless sacrifice.

Marriage Is Hard Work!

Unfortunately,
we tend to take better care
of our cars and houses
than we do our marriages.
We change the oil,
fill the tank,
check the tires,
and periodically tune up our cars.
We change light bulbs,
wash windows,
paint walls,

unplug toilets,
and re-roof our houses.
But what have we done lately
to take care of our marriage?

If you don't put
        the time
        the thought
        the effort
        and the tender loving care
into your marriage, it will fail.
I have spoken to thousands of people
who, at one time, insisted that
it would *never* happen to them.
But no one is immune—
not the president,
not the pastor,
not the kindest person in the world.
It's very simple—
if you don't take care of it,
it won't last.

We live in a world of
        hollow marriages
        and nasty divorces.
If you don't strengthen your relationship,
you two will become
just one more statistic of failure.
It doesn't matter if you've been married
five years or fifty years.
Love is not enough.
Good intentions are not enough.

Hard work is what strengthens marriages,
and God's grace is what
saves them.

So where do we start?
With understanding.
Trying to understand
    who you are
    who they are
    and how the two of you relate.
That is the beginning.

Start with questions,
for questions open up doors
and open up hearts
and open up communication.
As one author wrote,
Communication is the key to your marriage.

So ask questions—
questions about
    the past
    the future
    commitment
    conflict
    finances
    affection
    children
    God
    and romance.

Here are 101 major questions
and hundreds upon hundreds
of sub-questions
to help strengthen your marriage.
Take your time
and answer them
        patiently
        with thought and consideration.
Talk about your answers.
Discuss the questions.
Use this book to bring you closer together.

Remember—
        the more time
        and thought
        and effort
        and tender loving care
you put into your marriage,
the stronger your relationship will be.

WHAT WOULD OUR DREAM HOUSE BE LIKE?

What architectural style do you like?

☐ Victorian
☐ Colonial
☐ Chateau
☐ Spanish
☐ Tudor
☐ Cottage
☐ Adobe

☐ Ranch
☐ Log cabin
☐ Modern
☐ Japanese
☐ Arts and Crafts
☐ Bungalow
☐ Cape Cod

Where would you like to live?

☐ In a big city
☐ In the country
☐ In a suburban
  neighborhood
☐ In a small town
☐ By the mountains
☐ In the desert

☐ At the beach
☐ On a hill
☐ By a river
☐ On a farm
☐ Near a lake

2

WHAT IS YOUR FAVORITE KIND OF GIFT?

❧ What is the best gift you've ever received?

❧ What gift wasn't such a hit?

❧ What is the most creative gift you've received?

❧ What is the most romantic gift you've received?

3

*W*HAT *D*O *Y*OU *R*EMEMBER *A*BOUT *O*UR *F*IRST *D*ATE?

✤ Where did we go?

✤ Who invited whom? How was it planned?

✤ What did we talk about?

✤ What are some of your favorite and
not-so-favorite memories of it?

✤ What did we wear?

✤ Were you nervous?

✤ Did we kiss?

❦4❦

*W*HEN DID YOU FIRST DECIDE YOU WANTED TO MARRY ME?

❧ Where were you and what were you doing?

❧ What drew you to me?

❧ Did you think we were ready to get married?

❧ What did your parents and friends think of me?

❧ What do you remember about the proposal?

WHAT WAS OUR WEDDING LIKE?

❧ What was your favorite part of the ceremony?

❧ What made our wedding unique and special?

Location: _____

The Wedding Party: _____

_____

Colors: _____

Songs: _____

Type of flowers: _____

Food at the Reception: _____

_____

Minister: _____

Prayers: _____

Cake: _____

❧ What do you remember about our vows?

❧ What is your best memory of our wedding night?

6

*W*HAT WORDS DO YOU LIKE TO HEAR FROM ME?

These are the things I love to hear from you—

☐ *"I love you more every day."*
☐ *"You are wonderful."*
☐ *"I sure do appreciate you."*
☐ *"You're so special."*
☐ *"I'm so glad to be with you."*
☐ *"Good job."*
☐ *"What can I do to help?"*
☐ *"I missed you."*
☐ *"I'm sorry."*
☐ *"I was wrong."*
☐ *"How can I be a better partner?"*
☐ *"Thank you."*
☐ *"You look fantastic today."*
☐ *"You are the best thing that ever happened to me."*

❦ Which of these are easiest to say? Which are more difficult to say?

❦ What else would you like to hear from me?

∼∽ 7 ∽∼

*W*HAT ARE YOUR EARLIEST MEMORIES?

❧ What are some things you remember from long ago?

❧ How old were you?

❧ Where were you?

❧ Who were you with?

❧ What made these things special?

❧ How have these early memories shaped who you are?

8

*W*HAT HAVE BEEN THE HIGH POINTS OF YOUR LIFE?

Of your personal life: _____

Of your romantic life: _____

Of your social life: _____

Of your spiritual life: _____

Of your professional life: _____

Of your financial life: _____

Of your physical life: _____

Of your family life: _____

❧ Which of the above areas do you cherish the most?

   Why?

❧ Which of these do you think have had the most influence on who you are today?

❧ How can I encourage you in some of these areas? How do you think you can encourage me?

9

WHAT'S EASIER—
FORGIVING ME OR ASKING
ME TO FORGIVE YOU?

❧ Why is it easier?

❧ When is it not so easy?

❧ Have you ever found it very difficult or
almost impossible to forgive me?

What happened?

*Was there anything that finally made
forgiveness possible?*

What was it?

⊸ 10 ⊷

How Would You Describe the Family You Grew Up With?

🥀 What are their strong points?

🥀 Which of these have you inherited?

🥀 What are their weak points?

🥀 Which of these have you inherited?

🥀 What is your place in order of birth?

🥀 How do you think it affected you?

🥀 How similar is our marriage to your parents' marriage?

🥀 How is our marriage different from your parents' marriage?

🥀 What traditions from your parents would you like to continue?

🥀 What traditions of our own would you like to create?

~ 11 ~

WHAT WERE YOUR BEST SUBJECTS IN SCHOOL?

What subjects did you do well in?

☐ Math
☐ Science
☐ History
☐ Drama
☐ Physical Education
☐ Art
☐ Band/Orchestra
☐ Computers
☐ Photography
☐ Home Economics
☐ Social Studies
☐ English

☐ Economics/personal finance
☐ Geography
☐ Speech/Debate
☐ Foreign Language
☐ Psychology
☐ Choir
☐ Journalism
☐ Industrial Arts
☐ Drafting/Design
☐ Other: _____

✿ What were your worst subjects?
   Why?

✿ How do you think you would do in these subjects today?

~ 12 ~

$\mathcal{W}$HAT RECURRING DREAMS HAVE YOU HAD?

During childhood?

During adolescence?

During adulthood?

❧ What is the most frightening nightmare you've ever had?

How old were you when you first had it?

Where were you in the nightmare?

Who else was in it?

Who have you told about it?

Did it go away?

❧ 13 ❧

𝒲HO'S THE MOST INFLUENTIAL PERSON IN YOUR LIFE?

Why is he or she so influential?

❧ Who do you admire the most?

What qualities about this person do you admire?

❧ Who have been your heroes?

*Cinema heroes:*_____

*Historical heroes:*_____

*Literary heroes:*_____

Musical heroes: _____

*Spiritual heroes:*_____

*Sports heroes:*_____

Other heroes: _____

❧ Do you think you've been a hero in someone else's life? How so?

∞14∞

WHICH STAGE IS OUR MARRIAGE CURRENTLY IN?

Which one of these stages best describes our relationship right now?[1]

☐ Fantasy Stage: *"This is wonderful! My partner is everything I dreamed of and more!"*

☐ Surprise Stage: *"This isn't exactly what I expected. Oh, well, it's probably just a phase."*

☐ Questioning Stage: *"What did I get myself into? Did I make a mistake?"*

☐ Disillusioned Stage: *"I can't believe I'm in this situation! Why was I so blind?"*

☐ Realistic Stage: *"This relationship has some strong points and some weak points. It's not perfect, but neither am I."*

☐ Stabilized Stage: *"This relationship is made of two struggling people, and if we work together we can truly be happy and fulfilled."*

✿ Which stage were we in the longest?

Why?

✿ How can we get to the stabilized stage?

~~15~~

WHAT WERE THE BEST PARTS OF OUR HONEYMOON?

What do you remember about where we went?

Which part did you like best?

If we could go again, what should we do differently?

What is your most romantic memory of our honeymoon?

Did we go on a second honeymoon?

If we have, where and when did we go?

If we haven't, where and when would you like to go?

❦ 16 ❦

Ẇhat Is the Biggest Frustration in Our Relationship?

Which of these things apply to our relationship?

☐ Selfishness   ☐ Laziness

☐ Disappointment   ☐ Hurt

☐ Unhappiness   ☐ Busyness

☐ Negativity   ☐ Fear

☐ Boredom   ☐ Distance

❧ How often do each of these affect our relationship?

❧ When do we tend to slip into one of these traps?

❧ How do we treat each other when we've slipped into these traps?

17

Which Couple Would You Like to Dress Up as for a Masquerade Party?

Which of these famous couples could you see us portraying?

- ☐ Adam and Eve
- ☐ Superman and Lois Lane
- ☐ Peter Pan and Wendy
- ☐ Romeo and Juliet
- ☐ Aladdin and Jasmine
- ☐ Bogie and Bacall
- ☐ Boaz and Ruth
- ☐ Joe DiMaggio and Marilyn Monroe
- ☐ Tarzan and Jane
- ☐ Captain and Tenille
- ☐ Laura Ingalls and Almanzo Wilder
- ☐ Bonnie and Clyde
- ☐ Scarlett O'Hara and Rhett Butler
- ☐ John F. and Jackie Kennedy
- ☐ F. Scott Fitzgerald and Zelda
- ☐ Roy Rogers and Dale Evans
- ☐ Anthony and Cleopatra
- ☐ Mary and Joseph
- ☐ Robert Browning and Elizabeth Barret Browning

Which couple are we most like? *Why?*

Which couple are we least like? *Why?*

❧ 18 ❧

*W*HEN DID WE LAST TALK ABOUT…?

Our childhood: _____

Our wedding: _____

Our musical tastes: _____

Our political beliefs: _____

Our finances: _____

Our hopes and dreams: _____

Our fears: _____

Our sexual relationship: _____

Our religious beliefs: _____

Our dream vacation: _____

Our future: _____

❧ Were these talks positive or negative? Why?

❧ What are some other things you'd like for us to talk about?

⇜ 19 ⇝

WHAT DOES COMMITMENT MEAN TO YOU?

🌹 Why do you think commitment is important?

🌹 Are you more or less committed to me than you were during our first year of marriage?

🌹 In what ways should our marriage be total and timeless?

❧ 20 ❧

*W*HAT *W*AS *Y*OUR *P*ARENTS' *M*ARRIAGE *L*IKE?

❧ What was the best part of their marriage?

❧ Do you think their commitment was total and timeless?

Why or why not?

❧ How does their marriage influence your view of commitment?

❧ Would you want a relationship like theirs?

Why or why not?

∾21∾

*H*OW ARE WE COMPATIBLE?

Think of five ways we're compatible—

1. _____

2. _____

3. _____

4. _____

5. _____

❧ How do these ways strengthen our
relationship?

⮷⮷22⮷⮷

*H*OW ARE WE
INCOMPATIBLE?

Think of five ways we're not compatible—

1. _____

2. _____

3. _____

4. _____

5. _____

❧ How do we respond to these
incompatibilities?

✦23✦

*I*N WHAT WAYS ARE WE DIFFERENT FROM EACH OTHER?

❦ Which of these personality traits best fits us? (Circle hers, underline his)

Extrovert	or	Introvert
Leaper	or	Looker
Outliner	or	Detailer
Spender	or	Saver
Planner	or	Flexer
Scurrier	or	Ambler
Thinker	or	Feeler
Dreamer	or	Worker
Collector	or	Tosser

❦ Which one of these traits do you appreciate the most about me?

❦ Which one of these traits frustrates you the most about me?

❦ What do we usually do when one of these differences creates a conflict in our marriage?

∝⌒24⌒∝

ᾧHAT "RIGHTS" IN OUR RELATIONSHIP ARE MOST IMPORTANT TO YOU?

Mark the ones that matter most—[2]

☐ *The right to feel:*   *Respecting my partner's emotions in a nonjudgmental, compassionate way.*

☐ *The right to know:*   *Providing my partner with honest and accurate information about things that affect him or her.*

☐ *The right to be heard:*   *Listening to my partner with my full attention and taking what he or she says seriously.*

☐ *The right to personal space:*   *Realizing that, at times, my partner needs physical and/or emotional space; respecting his or her privacy and allowing personal space.*

✄ Which of these rights do you honor best?

✄ Which of these do you find difficult to honor?

∼∽25∼∽

*H*OW DO WE
SHOW RESPECT
FOR EACH OTHER?

❧ How do our attitudes show respect for
each other?

How do they not show respect?

❧ How do our words show respect?

How do they not show respect?

❧ How do our actions show respect?

How do they not show respect?

❧ How can we do a better job of showing
respect for each other?

~26~

*W*HAT KIND OF LOVE DO WE DEMONSTRATE THE MOST IN OUR MARRIAGE?

Mark the types that we show the most—

☐ *Practical love.*   ☐ *Romantic love.*

☐ *Sacrificial love.*   ☐ *Friendship love.*

☐ *Protective love.*   ☐ *Playful love.*

❧ What type of love do we demonstrate the least? *Why?*

❧ Which is the most important to you? *Why?*

27

*H*OW DO WE LISTEN TO EACH OTHER?

❧ When do you listen the best?

❧ When do you have trouble listening?

❧ Do you think that I am a good listener?

❧ What keeps you from fully listening to me?

∽28∽

*H*OW GOOD ARE YOU AT GIVING COMPLIMENTS?

How good are you at giving compliments . . .

About possessions: "I like what you have."
About appearance: "I like how you look."
About performance: "I like what you do."
About character: "I like who you are."

❀ In which area do you give the most compliments?

❀ In which area do you give the least?

❀ When is the last time you gave me a compliment in each of those areas?

❀ Write down two compliments about me in each of these areas.

Possessions: 1._____
2._____

Appearance: 1._____
2._____

Performance: 1._____
2._____

Character: 1._____
2._____

29

What Has Been the Biggest Miscommunication We've Had in the Past Year?

- How did the miscommunication start?
- What was it about?
- How could we have avoided it?
- How did we resolve it?
- How can we communicate better next time?

❧30❧

WHAT ARE YOUR FAVORITES?

*Favorite restaurant:*_____

*Favorite car:*_____

*Favorite book:*_____

*Favorite animal:*_____

*Favorite song:*_____

*Favorite movie:*_____

*Favorite season:*_____

*Favorite flower:*_____

*Favorite color:*_____

*Favorite living figure:*_____

*Favorite historical figure:*_____

*Favorite ice cream:*_____

*Favorite sport:*_____

*Favorite place to go on a date:*_____

*Favorite park:*_____

*Favorite creative activity:*_____

31

WHAT IS THE NICEST THING I'VE EVER SAID TO YOU?

❧ When did I say it?

❧ What was your response?

❧ What is the nicest thing you've ever said to me?

❧ What motivated you to say it?

❧ How did I respond?

❦ 32 ❦

How Many Hours Each Week Do We Talk with Each Other?

❧ Who do you think does the most talking?

❧ What are some things we like to talk about?

❧ How would you describe most of our talks?

☐ Monologue   ☐ Dialogue

☐ Lecture   ☐ Interaction

☐ Correction   ☐ Conflict

☐ Sermon   ☐ Discussion

☐ Debate   ☐ Interruption

☐ Chat   ☐ Confrontation

☐ Conference   ☐ Gabfest

☐ Adventure   ☐ Heart-to-heart

∞‍33∞

WHAT TOPICS ARE DIFFICULT FOR US TO DISCUSS?

Mark the things that are hard to talk about—

☐ Sex   ☐ Money

☐ Feelings   ☐ God

☐ Friends   ☐ Relatives

☐ Failures   ☐ Sins

☐ Imperfections   ☐ Complaints

☐ Job   ☐ Goals

☐ Children   ☐ Expectations

☐ Compliments   ☐ Communication

🌹 What would make it easier to talk about these things?

🌹 Have we ever kept any secrets from each other? What were they? Why did we keep them secret?

🌹 What can we do to make it easier to share secrets?

❦ 34 ❦

WHAT IS ROMANTIC TO YOU?

Most romantic song:_____

Most romantic movie:_____

Most romantic place:_____

Most romantic restaurant:_____

Most romantic color:_____

Most romantic perfume:_____

Most romantic cologne:_____

Most romantic flower:_____

Most romantic beverage:_____

Most romantic book:_____

Most romantic clothing:_____

Most romantic memory:_____

Most romantic thing to say:_____

Most romantic time of day:_____

Most romantic type of touch:_____

Most romantic season:_____

Most romantic vacation destination:_____

Most romantic dessert:_____

Most romantic surprise:_____

Most romantic poem:_____

❦35❦

WHAT HAVE I DONE THAT HAS UPSET YOU THE MOST?

❧ What have you done to resolve it?

❧ What have I done to resolve it?

❧ What have you done that has upset me the most?

❧ What have I done to resolve it?

❧ What have you done to resolve it?

36

WHAT IS MOST LIKELY TO TRIGGER OUR ANGER?

Mark the things that upset you most—

☐ Frustration   ☐ Loss

☐ Fear   ☐ Hurt

☐ Injustice   ☐ Embarrassment

☐ Disappointment   ☐ Insecurity

☐ Anxiety   ☐ Betrayal

❧ When was the last time you got angry?

❧ Did the anger make the situation better or worse? *Why?*

❧ What is a healthier way to deal with our anger?

37

$\mathcal{W}$HEN WAS THE LAST TIME WE LAUGHED TOGETHER?

❧ How would you describe my sense of humor?

❧ What things do you find the funniest?

Your funniest TV show: _____

Your funniest joke: _____

Your funniest movie: _____

Your funniest person: _____

Your funniest memory: _____

Your funniest activity: _____

Your funniest story: _____

Your funniest picture: _____

Your funniest song: _____

Your funniest cartoon: _____

≈≈38≈≈

Do You Believe in God?

Why or why not?

🌹 If you do believe in God, which of the following attributes describe Him?

☐ *Omnipresent:* God is everwhere.

☐ *Omniscient:* God knows everything.

☐ *Omnipotent:* God is all powerful.

☐ *Infinite:* God has no limitations.

☐ *Sovereign:* God has ultimate control over everything.

☐ *Good:* God is morally perfect and is the ultimate yard-stick for every virtue.

☐ *Loving:* God cares intimately about every individual

🌹 How are your beliefs about God similar to or different from your parents' beliefs?

39

How Often Do We Encourage and Build Up Each Other?

❧ Are you most likely to encourage me with words or actions?

❧ When was the last time I encouraged you or built you up?

What was the occasion?

What did I say or do?

How did my encouragement affect the situation?

❧ What encourages you the most?

☙40☙

$\mathscr{H}$OW WOULD YOU DESCRIBE MOST OF OUR FIGHTS WITH EACH OTHER?

Mark the ones that apply—

☐ Hurtful   ☐ Helpful

☐ Loud   ☐ Short

☐ Intense   ☐ Abusive

☐ Educational   ☐ Angry

☐ Valuable   ☐ Petty

☐ Confusing   ☐ Threatening

☐ Respectful   ☐ Frustrating

☐ Unnecessary   ☐ Fair

☐ Unfair   ☐ Exhausting

✄ When are our fights most likely to start?

✄ Where are they most likely to start?

✄ How are they most likely to start?

✄ How do we generally end them?

✑41✑

How Often Do We Fight with Each Other?

✿ In which of the following areas do we have the most conflicts?

☐ Parenting   ☐ Distribution of household chores

☐ Relatives and in-laws   ☐ Communication styles

☐ Money management   ☐ Expression of affection and sexuality

☐ Friendships outside marriage

✿ In which of these areas do we agree most of the time?

✿ What would help us agree on more things?

42

*H*OW DO WE RESOLVE CONFLICTS IN OUR RELATIONSHIP?

🌹 How long does it take us to resolve conflicts?

🌹 Which of us is the most likely to give in to the other?

Does the other partner ever resent this?

🌹 What three rules can we create to help our conflicts be more helpful and less hurtful?

1. _____

2. _____

3. _____

∽43∽

HOW DO OUR CHILDREN AFFECT OUR MARRIAGE?

❧ How has our social life changed since we had children?

❧ How has our sexual life changed since we had children?

❧ How has our communication changed since we had children?

❧ How has our spiritual life changed since we had children?

❧ How have our goals and dreams changed since we had children?

❧ What have our children added to our relationship?

∽∾44∿∾

How Would We Grade Ourselves As Parents?

❧ What is your philosophy of parenting?

Do we both agree with this philosophy?

❧ What is your approach to discipline?

Do we both agree with this approach?

❧ Which of us is stricter with the children?

How does this affect our relationship?

❧ Which of us spends more time with the children?

How does this affect our relationship?

∼∽45∾∼

$\mathcal{W}$HAT VIRTUES ARE MOST IMPORTANT TO PASS ON TO OUR CHILDREN?

Mark your top three virtues—

☐ Honesty   ☐ Respect

☐ Courage   ☐ Self-discipline

☐ Kindness   ☐ Compassion

☐ Patience   ☐ Humility

☐ Spirituality   ☐ Fairness

☐ Hard work   ☐ Obedience

☐ Purity   ☐ Responsibility

❧ Why are these virtues important to you?

❧ What can we do to give our children these virtues?

❧ What makes it difficult to build these virtues into our children?

～46～

HOW DO WE SHARE OUR HOUSEHOLD CHORES?

❧ Which one of us does the following jobs?
(Circle hers and underline his; box
the ones that we both do)

Car care and repair
Child discipline
Correspondence
Entertaining
Financial provision
Garbage and recycling
General house cleaning
Interior decorating
Major home repairs
Packing for vacations
Pet care
Shopping (food, clothes,
   interior furnishings,
   appliances, cars, etc.)

Child care
Child education
Dishes
Financial planning
Food preparation
Gardening
Household maintenance
Laundry
Miscellaneous errands
Paying bills
Spiritual direction
Vacation planning
Yard work

❧ Do you think these jobs are distributed
   fairly?

❧ What adjustments should we make?

∽47∽

How Do You Feel About Your In-Laws?

Do you like them?

Do you respect them?

Do you trust them?

Do you enjoy spending time with them?

❧ How often do you see them?

What do you do when you're together?

What do you talk about when you're together?

How often do you like to see them?

❧ What do you admire most about them?

❧ What frustrates you most about them?

❧ Does your relationship with your in-laws create conflict between us?

How can this conflict be resolved?

❦ 48 ❦

*W*HAT AREA OF OUR HOUSE DO YOU ENJOY THE MOST?

Mark the rooms that you like best—

☐ Family room   ☐ Kitchen
☐ Bedroom   ☐ Hot tub/Sauna
☐ Bathroom   ☐ Laundry room
☐ Storage room   ☐ Entertainment room
☐ Sewing room/   ☐ Den/Library
    Hobby room   ☐ Exercise room
☐ Dining room   ☐ Deck/Patio
☐ Garage   ☐ Backyard
☐ Porch   ☐ Garden room
☐ Guest room   ☐ Basement
☐ Attic   ☐ Greenhouse
☐ Home office   ☐ Living room
☐ Nursery

❧ What area of our house do you enjoy least? *Why?*

❧ How can we make the rooms in our home more appealing?

∽∽49∽∽

WHAT IS THE BEST ADVICE YOU'VE EVER HEARD?

*About life:*_____

*About God:*_____

*About marriage:*_____

*About children:*_____

*About money:*_____

*About sex:*_____

*About work:*_____

*About fun:*_____

*About friends:*_____

*About leaving a legacy:*_____

❧ What is the least helpful advice you've ever heard about these things?

∞50∞

*W*HAT IS THE TOUGHEST RUT OUR MARRIAGE EVER EXPERIENCED?

❧ How did we get in it?

❧ How long were we in it?

❧ Which one of us first noticed it?

How did that partner let the other know about it?

How did the other respond to it?

❧ How did we get out of it?

❧ What did we learn from it?

∞51∞

WHAT FORM OF UNHEALTHY TALK DO YOU ENGAGE IN?

Mark the ones that apply—

☐ Swearing
☐ Negative
   statements
☐ Blaming
☐ Exaggeration
☐ Embarrassing
   statements
☐ Coarse joking

☐ Sarcasm
☐ Thoughtless
   words
☐ Overtalking
☐ Manipulation
☐ Belittling
☐ Name calling
☐ Hurtful words

✄ When is the last time you used any of these forms of unhealthy talk?

✄ How do I respond when you talk like that?

✄ What do you feel when you hear these things?

≈≈52≈≈

How Deeply Do We Communicate with Each Other?

Mark the levels that apply to our marriage—

☐ Superficial level   ☐ Fact level

☐ Opinion level   ☐ Emotion level

☐ Everything level

❧ Are you satisfied with our level of communication?

❧ Do you think I am satisfied with our level of communication?

❧ What couple do we know who communicates deeply with each other?

How do they do it?

How do you think we can do it?

∽ 53 ∾

WHAT PREVENTS US FROM COMMUNICATING MORE?

Mark the reasons that apply to our marriage—

☐ Don't know what to say.
☐ Don't feel like we have anything worthwhile to say.
☐ Afraid of starting a fight.
☐ Afraid of sounding foolish.
☐ Don't know how to put thoughts and feelings into the right words.
☐ Takes too much effort.
☐ Don't feel like partner will truly listen.
☐ Too busy to talk.
☐ Afraid of being too vulnerable.
☐ Believe "talking will get you into trouble."

❧ Which of us is more of a communicator?

How does this affect our relationship?

❧ Who in our extended families talks the most and who is the quietest?

∼∙54∙∼

How Often Do We Disagree About Money?

❦ What is the most foolish purchase you've made since we got married?

❦ What is the most satisfying purchase you've made?

❦ What is the most foolish purchase I've made since we got married?

❦ What is the most satisfying purchase I've made?

❦ What purchase created the most conflict between us?

❦ If one of us wants to make a purchase and the other disagrees with it, how do we resolve the issue?

~~55~~

*W*HAT KIND OF MOVIES DO YOU LIKE TO WATCH?

Mark the genres that you like to watch with me—

☐ Romance
☐ Historical
☐ Science-fiction/
   Fantasy
☐ Western
☐ Documentary
☐ Family
☐ Musical
☐ Cartoon/
   Animation
☐ Slapstick

☐ Military
☐ Comedy
☐ Drama
☐ Classic
☐ Action/Adventure
☐ Mystery/Suspense
☐ Foreign
☐ Christian/Inspirational
☐ Children's
☐ Silent
☐ Nature Story

❧ What kind of movies do you like to watch when you're alone?

❧ What kind of movies do you like to watch when you're with friends?

∽⟋56⟍∼

*W*HEN IS THE LAST TIME WE DID THESE THINGS?

*Held hands in public:*_____

Whispered something sweet to
   each other: _____

*Kissed outside the bedroom:*_____

*Hugged outside the bedroom:*_____

Gave each other a back rub, leg rub,
   or foot rub: _____

*Snuggled on the sofa:*_____

*Put your arm around my shoulder:*_____

*Held each other close:*_____

*Said "I love you":*_____

*Placed your hand on my thigh:*_____

❦ Who initiated the contact?

❦ How did it feel?

❦ How often did you see your parents doing
   these things?

❦ How did you feel when you saw them
   being tender with each other?

✧57✧

HOW DO WE SEE
SEXUALITY DIFFERENTLY?

🥀 How comfortable are you discussing
  sexuality with me?

🥀 Do you think our sexual relationship is
  more important to one of us than it is
  to the other?

  In what ways?

  *Why do you think we have this
  difference?*

🥀 How does our sexual relationship
  strengthen our marriage?

∾58∾

*W*HAT ARE YOUR EXPECTATIONS FOR ME IN THE NEXT YEAR?

*Educational:*_____

*Financial:*_____

*Occupational:*_____

*Spiritual:*_____

*Personal:*_____

*Marital:*_____

*Parental:*_____

*Sexual:*_____

*Intellectual:*_____

*Emotional:*_____

*Social:*_____

*Recreational:*_____

What are your expectations for us in the next five years?

The next ten years?

∞59∞

Who Is Your Closest Friend Besides Me?

🌹 How long have you known each other?

🌹 Why are you friends?

🌹 What do I think about this friend?

🌹 What do your outside friendships give you that our marriage doesn't?

In what ways is this healthy?

60

$\mathcal{W}$HAT CLOSE FRIENDS DO YOU HAVE OF THE OPPOSITE SEX?

How long have you known each other?

Why are you friends?

What do I think about this friendship?

❧ At what point do you think a friendship with someone of the opposite sex can become a threat to our marriage?

What are the warning signs that we should notice?

Do we currently notice any of these warning signs?

❧ If I asked you to end this friendship, would you be willing to end it?

Why or why not?

61

What Animals Are You Most Like When You're Angry?

Mark the ones that describe you—

☐ *turtle:*	You withdraw inside yourself.
☐ *deer:*	You get away as fast as you can.
☐ *shark:*	You go for blood.
☐ *donkey:*	You stand your ground and don't budge.
☐ *monkey:*	You jump up and down while making a lot of noise.
☐ *chameleon:*	You change your colors to fit in.
☐ *house cat:*	You snuggle up and try to make everything okay.
☐ *python:*	You put on the squeeze until you get what you want.
☐ *beaver:*	You work hard to calmly resolve the situation.
☐ *elephant:*	You give in, but you never forget.

Where did you learn to be like these animals?

What animals am I most like when I'm angry?

Where do you think I learned to be like this animal?

∞§62∞

$\mathcal{W}$HAT HABITS DO I HAVE THAT FRUSTRATE YOU?

List three of these habits—

1. _____

2. _____

3. _____

How do you deal with these?

What habits do I have that endear me to you?

1. _____

2. _____

3. _____

How have these helped our marriage?

∾∾63∾∾

WHAT HAVE BEEN YOUR GREATEST DISAPPOINTMENTS?

In life:_____

In school:_____

In work:_____

In family:_____

In finances:_____

In friendships:_____

In churches:_____

In yourself:_____

✖ What have you done to either change, manage, or accept these disappointments?

～64～

Ｗhat Styles of Music Do You Enjoy the Most?

Mark the ones that you like to listen to—

☐ Popular (Top 40)   ☐ Rock

☐ Alternative   ☐ Country

☐ Heavy metal   ☐ Rhythm and Blues

☐ Contemporary   ☐ Rap

　　Christian/Gospel   ☐ Classical

☐ Easy Listening   ☐ Big Band

☐ Jazz   ☐ Broadway show tunes

✎ Which styles do you like the least?

✎ What musician or group do you enjoy the most?

✎ What song would you call "our song"?

∞65∞

*H*OW DO YOU FEEL ABOUT YOUR PARENTS?

Do you like them?
Do you respect them?
Do you trust them?
Do you enjoy spending time with them?

❧ How often do you see them?

What do you do when you're together?

What do you talk about when you're together?

How often do you like to see them?

❧ What do you admire most about them?

❧ What frustrates you most about them?

❧ Is your relationship with your parents a point of conflict between us?

If it is, how can we resolve this conflict?

～66～

WHEN HURT, WHICH OF THE FOLLOWING PROMISES ARE EASIEST FOR YOU TO KEEP?

Mark the ones that are easiest—[3]

☐ You will no longer dwell on your hurt.

☐ You will not bring up your hurt and use it against me.

☐ You will not talk to others about your hurt.

☐ You will not allow your hurt to stand between us or hinder our relationship.

🌤 Which promises are the most difficult to keep?

Why?

🌤 What would make it easier for you to keep these promises?

~~67~~

*W*HEN YOU'VE WRONGED ME, HOW DIFFICULT IS IT TO DO THE FOLLOWING...?

*Acknowledge your guilt:*_____

*Recognize my hurt:*_____

*Ask for my forgiveness:*_____

*Change your hurtful behavior:*_____

*Implement safeguards for our future:*_____

*Make restitution:*_____

🌹 What motivates you to do each of these things?

🌹 What prevents you from doing these things?

🌹 When is the last time you've done each of these things?

68

What Aspects of the Arts Do You Enjoy?

Mark the ones that you like—

- ☐ Theater
- ☐ Dance
- ☐ Poetry
- ☐ Sculpture
- ☐ Textiles
- ☐ Gardening
- ☐ Painting and Drawing (Visual Art)
- ☐ Music
- ☐ Literature
- ☐ Photography
- ☐ Cinematography
- ☐ Pottery
- ☐ Carpentry
- ☐ Other

In which of the arts have you participated?

In which would you *like* to participate?

✤69✤

IN WHAT AREAS DO WE HAVE DIFFERENT COMFORT ZONES?

🌹 How would you describe our comfort zones in different situations?

🌹 Are we able to discuss these differences?

🌹 Do we feel listened to when we discuss these differences?

🌹 Are we satisfied with how we've resolved these differences?

～∾70∾～

*W*HEN WAS THE LAST TIME YOU DID SOMETHING SPECIAL FOR ME?

Rubbed my back: _____

Sent me flowers: _____

Kissed me: _____

Gave me a card for no particular reason: _____

Surprised me with dinner: _____

Placed my preference above yours: _____

Called me up to wish me a great day: _____

Wrote me a love letter: _____

Bought my favorite ice cream: _____

Washed my car: _____

What would you like me to do for you?

∽∾71∽∾

LAST YEAR, WHAT DID I GIVE YOU ON THE FOLLOWING DAYS?

Christmas: _____

Birthday: _____

Wedding Anniversary: _____

Valentine's Day: _____

Mother's or Father's Day: _____

❦ How did you receive each gift?

❦ What did you think about the gifts?

∽∽72∽∽

WHEN WAS THE LAST TIME WE WENT ON A DATE?

What did we do?

Who initiated the date?

Did we have a good time?

What reasons keep us from going on dates more often?

☐ Our lives are too busy.

☐ We don't have the money.

☐ We enjoy doing different things.

☐ Our children keep us too busy.

☐ Our jobs keep us too busy.

☐ We can't agree on what to do.

How can we overcome these obstacles?

✺73✺

*I*N WHAT AREAS OF TOGETHERNESS ARE WE THE MOST SUCCESSFUL?

Rank these (1–8) in order of how successful we are at them—[4]

____ *Emotional:*	Being tuned into each each other's emotions.
____ *Intellectual:*	Sharing thoughts, ideas, opinions, and beliefs.
____ *Aesthetic:*	Enjoying the beauty and artistry of life.
____ *Recreational:*	Having fun as a couple.
____ *Work:*	Doing common, everyday tasks and chores as a team.
____ *Crisis:*	Leaning on each other when times are hard.
____ *Sexual:*	Bonding through physical closeness.
____ *Spiritual:*	Drawing closer to God and encouraging each other's faith.

✺ In which of the above areas do you want us to grow even closer? *Why?*

How do you think we can do this?

∾ 74 ∾

WHICH OF THE FOLLOWING EMOTIONS DO YOU EXPERIENCE THE MOST?

Mark the ones that you feel most often—

☐ Anger   ☐ Anxiety

☐ Boredom   ☐ Confusion

☐ Depression   ☐ Exhaustion

☐ Fear   ☐ Grief

☐ Guilt   ☐ Humiliation

☐ Hurt   ☐ Jealousy

☐ Joy   ☐ Loneliness

☐ Optimism   ☐ Peace

☐ Regret   ☐ Sadness

☐ Strength

✿ How can I know that you are feeling these emotions?

✿ How would you like me to respond to your emotions?

❧ 75 ❧

WHAT DO WE DO TO CREATE INTELLECTUAL TOGETHERNESS?

❧ When was the last time we read a book together? What book was it?

What did you enjoy the most about doing this?

❧ When was the last time we discussed a political, social, or philosophical issue together?

Did we agree or disagree?

Do you think our discussion was positive or negative?

❧ What is your philosophy of life?

How does this compare with my philosophy of life?

∽⟨76⟩∾

OF ALL THE PLACES WE'VE VISITED TOGETHER, WHICH WAS THE MOST BEAUTIFUL?

❧ Which place had the most influence on you?

Why?

❧ Which place brought us closest together?

Why?

❧ Would you like to return to any of these places?

Which ones?

❧ Where would you like to travel to someday?

⤬⤬77⤬⤬

*W*HAT WOULD YOUR PERFECT DAY BE LIKE?

❧ What would you do in the morning?

❧ What would you do in the afternoon?

❧ What would you do in the evening?

❧ Where would you go?

❧ What would you say?

❧ How would I be a part of this day?

~❦78❦~

WHAT COMMON, EVERYDAY TASK WOULD YOU RATHER DO WITH ME THAN DO ALONE?

Why?

❦ What tasks do you enjoy doing the most?

❦ What tasks are the hardest for you to do?

❦ What tasks do you think I enjoy the most?

❦ What tasks do you think are the hardest for me to do?

❦ What keeps us from doing more tasks together?

❦ What projects have we successfully worked on together?

∽∾79∽∾

WHAT IS THE BIGGEST CRISIS WE HAVE GONE THROUGH TOGETHER?

Would you say it pulled us apart or drew us closer together?

Why?

❧ What is the biggest personal crisis you've experienced since our marriage?

Were you able to share your emotions about this crisis with me?

Why or why not?

Was I there for you when you needed me? How did I help you?

❧ What is the biggest crisis your parents ever experienced?

How did they handle it?

How did it pull them apart or draw them closer together?

~~80~~

*H*OW WOULD YOU DESCRIBE OUR CURRENT SEXUAL RELATIONSHIP?

🌹 Do you think it is better or worse than it was a year ago?

🌹 Which of these things would improve your sexual satisfaction?

☐ Gentle initiation
☐ Increased frequency
☐ Increased touching
☐ Increased cuddling
☐ More romance
☐ Longer foreplay
☐ More variety
☐ Better communication
☐ Better hygiene
☐ Increased passion
☐ Romantic atmosphere
    (e.g., music, candlelight, perfume)
☐ Increased patience
☐ Different time of day

∞81∞

How Important Is Your Spiritual Life?

To you as an individual?

To you as a couple?

❧ Do you think our spiritual life divides or unites us?

Why?

❧ What have we done in the past week to develop spiritual togetherness?

❧ What would you like to do in the coming week to create spiritual togetherness?

82

$\mathcal{W}$HAT IS THE MOST ROMANTIC THING YOU'VE EVER DONE FOR ME?

How much planning did this take?

How did I respond?

❧ What is the most romantic thing I've ever done for you?

How much planning do you think it took?

How did you respond?

~~ 83 ~~

How Do You Respond to My Anger?

Mark the ways in which you respond—

☐ Ignore it
☐ Become frightened
☐ Stay away from it
☐ Worry
☐ Become angry
☐ Make peace at any price
☐ Talk it out

❧ How do you feel about your response?

❧ What do you think it says about our relationship?

❧ Is there a healthier way for us to respond to anger?

What way would this be?

84

$\mathcal{W}$HAT GIFTS FROM ME DO YOU TREASURE THE MOST?

Write down five gifts that you hold dear—

1. _____

2. _____

3. _____

4. _____

5. _____

What makes each of these gifts so special to you?

~~85~~

WHAT TYPE OF INTIMACY MAKES YOU FEEL THE CLOSEST TO ME?

Mark the things that make you feel closer— [5]

☐ Non-sexual touch

☐ Shared feelings

☐ Open communication

☐ Intellectual agreement

☐ Spiritual harmony

☐ Common values

☐ Imparted secrets

☐ Genuine understanding

☐ Mutual confidence

☐ Sensuous nearness

☐ Sexual pleasures

☐ Abiding trust

Which type of intimacy is the most difficult for you to achieve?

~86~

How Do You Like to Travel?

Mark the modes of transportation you enjoy the most—

☐ Train   ☐ Motorcycle

☐ Boat   ☐ Horse

☐ Airplane   ☐ On Foot

☐ Bicycle   ☐ Tandem bike

☐ Truck   ☐ Horse & carriage

☐ Bus   ☐ Hot air balloon

☐ Race car   ☐ Roller skates

☐ Van   ☐ Skis

✍ Where would you like to go via the above means of transportation?

∽✲87✲∽

How Do You Feel About Our Social Life?

🌺 What couples do we spend the most time with?

What do we usually do with them?

What draws you to these friendships?

Are they satisfying or do they create more work?

🌺 What other individuals or groups do we socialize with?

🌺 Who do we socialize with individually?

🌺 Who would you like to build a friendship with?

∽∾88∽∾

How Do We Celebrate Holidays?

Birthdays:_____

Anniversaries:_____

Valentine's Day: _____

Easter:_____

Mother's Day:_____

Memorial Day:_____

Father's Day:_____

Fourth of July: _____

Labor Day:_____

Veteran's Day: _____

Halloween:_____

Thanksgiving: _____

Christmas:_____

New Year's Eve:_____

New Year's Day: _____

❧ Do you like how we celebrate these holidays?

❧ How would you like to celebrate them
   differently?

～89～

WHAT SPORTS DO YOU ENJOY PARTICIPATING IN?

Mark the ones you like to do—

☐ Football   ☐ Basketball

☐ Soccer   ☐ Tennis

☐ Snow skiing   ☐ Water skiing

☐ Golf   ☐ Racquetball

☐ Track and Field   ☐ Bowling

☐ Baseball/Softball   ☐ Swimming

☐ Gymnastics   ☐ Running

☐ Ice skating   ☐ Volleyball

☐ Dancing (ballroom,
   ballet, square, western, etc.)

☐ Equestrian events

☐ Other:_____

✄ Which of these do you enjoy watching?

✄ Which sports do we like to do together?

⇜90⇝

WHAT IS THE WORST WAY I COULD BETRAY YOU?

🌿 How would you deal with this if it happened to you?

🌿 What is the most hurtful thing I could say to you?

🌿 What is the worst way you could betray me?

🌿 How would I deal with this if it happened to me?

🌿 What is the most hurtful thing you could say to me?

🌿 How can we make sure we don't betray each other?

WHAT WOULD YOU MOST LIKE TO EXPLORE TOGETHER?

Mark the places that sound fun to explore—

☐ A cave
☐ A museum
☐ A ghost town
☐ A gigantic bookstore
☐ A deserted island
☐ A snow-capped mountain
☐ A garden
☐ A city
☐ A jungle
☐ An underwater coral reef
☐ A desert
☐ Another country
☐ Another planet
☐ Another era

❧ Which of the above would you least like to explore together?

Why?

❧ Which of the above do you think you would like to explore, but I would not?

∼∽92∾∼

WHAT DOES YOUR SPIRITUAL JOURNEY LOOK LIKE?

❧ When did you first become aware of God?

❧ When have you felt closest to God?

❧ When have you felt most distant from God?

❧ How would you describe your relationship with God today?

❧❧93❧❧

*W*HAT DRAWS YOU CLOSER TO GOD?

Mark the ways that bring you closer—

☐ Appreciating nature
☐ Attending church
☐ Helping others
☐ Reading devotional
  or spiritual books
☐ Using your gifts
☐ Going to a Bible study
☐ Tithing
☐ Confessing your sins
☐ Memorizing
  Bible verses
☐ Doing good
☐ Giving to the poor
  and needy

☐ Praying
☐ Sharing your faith
☐ Reading your Bible
☐ Showing compassion
☐ Meditating
☐ Listening to spiritual
  music
☐ Speaking to those with
  similar beliefs
☐ Forgiving others
☐ Avoiding vices

❧ Which of these things do we do together?

❧ Which of these things could we do together?

❧ 94 ❧

*H*OW DO YOU RELATE TO GOD?

❧ How do you do the following?

*Sense God:*_____

Acknowledge God: _____

*Seek God:*_____

Trust God: _____

*Know God:*_____

Worship God: _____

*Respect God:*_____

*Honor God:*_____

Reflect upon God: _____

Serve God: _____

❧95❧

*W*HAT ARE YOUR NEEDS?

List your needs in order of priority (1 to 10).[6]

___ *Achievement:* to achieve a goal; overcome an obstacle or challenge.

___ *Affiliation:* draw near and interact with individuals or groups.

___ *Autonomy:* physical and/or emotional space; experience freedom; resist restriction.

___ *Control:* manage environment—including self, others, and things.

___ *Impact:* To be seen and heard.

___ *Growth:* explore and understand; ask or answer questions; gather information.

___ *Nurture:* assist others—support, protect, comfort, encourage, nurse.

___ *Play:* have fun; relax and enjoy.

___ *Security:* feel safe and supported; protected from harm and humiliation; be loved.

___ *Stimulation:* seek and enjoy sensory input— tactile, auditory, visual, olfactory, gustatory; to sexual.

❧ How well do I know your needs?

❧ How well do you know my needs?

⚜96⚜

*I*F YOU WON A MILLION DOLLARS, WHAT WOULD YOU DO WITH IT?

✤ How much would you put in savings or investments?

✤ How much would you use for purchases?

What would you buy?

Why would you buy these things?

✤ How much would you give to church or charities?

✤ How much would you use to buy gifts?

For whom?

What would you buy them?

✤ Do we agree on how the money would be used?

Which of the above would create the most conflict?

❧97❧

How Do You Respond to Hurt?

Mark the emotions that apply—

☐ With shock   ☐ With silence

☐ With acceptance   ☐ With depression

☐ With mistrust   ☐ With confrontation

☐ With withdrawal   ☐ With anger

☐ With suppression   ☐ With forgiveness

❧ What is the greatest hurt you've ever experienced?

When did it happen?

Who hurt you?

How have you dealt with it?

～❀98❀～

*W*HAT HAS BEEN THE HAPPIEST YEAR OF OUR MARRIAGE?

Why was this year so happy?

❧ Which was the worst year?
   Why?

❧ Which year was the most eventful?
   Why?

❧ Which year was the most romantic?
   Why?

*W*HICH OF OUR FRIENDS DO YOU FEEL THE LEAST COMFORTABLE WITH?

❧ What about this friend bothers you?

☐ *They're a negative influence.*

☐ *They're too demanding.*

☐ *They take advantage of you.*

☐ *They're hurtful to you.*

☐ *They undermine our marriage.*

☐ *They have a negative attitude.*

❧ Which of these reasons bothers you the most?

❧ If I asked you not to see this friend any-more, would you respect my request?

Why or why not?

∼∞100∞∼

*W*HAT MOMENT IN OUR MARRIAGE HAS BROUGHT YOU THE MOST JOY?

Why is this moment so special to you?

🌹 What moment in our marriage do you think brought me the most joy?

Why do you think that is so special to me?

🌹 If this were the last day of your life, what would we do together?

What would you want to say?

Where would you want to go?

∽101∾

WHAT MARITAL ADVICE WOULD YOU LIKE TO PASS ON TO OUR CHILDREN AND GRANDCHILDREN?

❧ How will they remember our marriage after we're gone?

❧ Why do you think they'll remember this?

❧ What positive things will they recall about our relationship?

❧ What negative things will they recall?

❧ What will they remember that might give them a happier and stronger marriage?

ENDNOTES

1. Steve Stephens, *Marriage: Experience the Best* (Portland, OR: Vision House, 1995), pp. 19-20.

2. George Bach and Ronald Deutsch, *Stop! You're Driving Me Crazy* (New York: Berkeley Books, 1979), pp. 55-130.

3. Ken Sande, *The Peacemaker: A Biblical Guide to Resolving Personal Conflict* (Grand Rapids, MI: Baker Books), p. 164.

4. Steve Stephens, *Marriage: Experience the Best* (Portland, OR: Vision House, 1995), pp. 211-231.

5. Ed Wheat and Gloria Perkins, *Love Life for Every Married Couple* (Grand Rapids, MI: Zondervan, 1980), pp. 133-134.

6. This is based on the theory and works of Henry A. Murray as presented in Calvin S. Hall and Gardner Lindzey, *Theories of Personality*, 2d ed. (New York: John Wiley and Sons, 1970), pp. 174-180.

Promise The Best

Marriage is not as easy
as you thought in the beginning.
The two of you are different people
than when you
first spoke your vows.
There have been
surprises and disappointments,
joys and tragedies,
humor and hurt.
Through it all,
you've made it this far.

Some of you have strong relationships
that you want to
make stronger.
Some of you struggle with difficult
relationships;
you aggravate and avoid
each other,
but you wish you could recapture
the spark you once had.
Some of you exist in dead relationships;
inertia and habit
provide the illusion of marriage
with none of the intimacy,
and you crave a single
meaningful touch.

Others of you have almost lost your
relationships;
    separation and dissolution
    seem inevitable,
    you don't know how to stop them,
    or maybe you aren't even sure
    you want to.
But whatever your situation,
you can promise the best.
I want you to have a
    strong marriage.
I don't want you to be
    stuck, miserable, divorced.
Hollow marriages and nasty divorces
    surround us.
You started out with so much love,
but time has taken its toll.
    The emotion,
    physical attraction,
    and sexual chemistry
that pulled you together has changed.
And if you aren't strong,
    promises are broken
    dreams are broken
    families are broken.
Hollow marriages and nasty divorces
make miserable, bitter, tragic people.

But there is *good news!*
If you've asked deep questions . . .
If you're as honest as you can be . . .

If you're determined to promise the
best . . . then you can have
    a great marriage.

Being the best partner possible
is not always easy.
At times it's not fair.
At times it hurts.
At times it's lonely.
It involves choosing
to love your partner
whether they deserve it
    or not.
It involves leaning on God
through good times and bad.
It involves an initial life-changing vow
followed by a procession of
    small
    simple
    selfless actions.
An initial vow began your marriage.
The following fifty promises
can strengthen your marriage.

1. Start each day with a kiss. 2. Wear your wedding rings at all times. 3. Date once a week. 4. Accept differences. 5. Be polite. 6. Be gentle. 7. Give gifts. 8. Smile often. 9. Touch. 10. Talk about dreams. 11. Choose a song that can be "your song." 12. Give back rubs. 13. Laugh together. 14. Send a card for no reason. 15. Do what they want before they ask. 16. Listen. 17. Encourage. 18. Do it their way. 19. Know their needs. 20. Fix their favorite breakfast. 21. Compliment them twice a day. 22. Call them. 23. Slow down. 24. Hold hands. 25. Cuddle. 26. Ask their opinion. 27. Show respect. 28. Welcome them home. 29. Look your best for them. 30. Wink at them. 31. Celebrate birthdays in a big way. 32. Apologize. 33. Forgive. 34. Set up a romantic getaway. 35. Ask, "What can I do to make you happier?" 36. Be positive. 37. Be kind. 38. Be vulnerable. 39. Respond quickly to their requests. 40. Talk about your love. 41. Reminisce about your favorite times together. 42. Treat their friends and relatives with courtesy. 43. Send flowers every Valentine's Day and anniversary. 44. Admit when you are wrong. 45. Be sensitive to their sexual desires. 46. Pray for them daily. 47. Watch sunsets together. 48. Say "I love you" frequently. 49. End each day with a hug. 50. Seek outside help when you need it.

These fifty promises
demonstrate who you are.
They move love from a feeling,
which comes and goes
like rain in the springtime,
to a commitment,
which steers steady on its
    course.

These are not promises
to be tried once or twice
and then tossed away.
They are promises
to be repeated often
with joy and enthusiasm.
For with God's grace
they will help strengthen
your marriage,
giving the two of you
a peace and happiness
that will last
    a lifetime.

Other Good
Harvest House Reading

LET HER KNOW YOU LOVE HER
by Bill Farrel

What man couldn't use some encouragement in romancing his wife? This little book contains numerous creative, encouraging ways for husbands to romance the leading ladies in their lives.

LOVE TO LOVE YOU
by Bill Farrel

Spark your relationship with these recipes for romance and one-of-a-kind relationship enhancers for Christian couples in love. Bill and Pam Farrel, who have been married for almost 18 years, share ways to build romantic traditions and plan fun, inexpensive dates.

QUIET TIMES FOR COUPLES
by H. Norman Wright

Designed to stimulate genuinely open communication between husband and wife, each day's devotion makes it easy for couples to share about the deeper parts of their lives.

QUIET MOMENTS FOR COUPLES
by H. Norman Wright

An inviting collection of inspirational reflections on love. Beautifully illustrated and calligraphied, it is a perfect gift for engagements, marriages, anniversaries, and more.